Hodgenville, Kentucky

AFTER, the Revolution, the Lincoln family moved from Virginia across the mountains into the frontier region of Kentucky between 1782 and 1784. Thomas Lincoln, father of the future President, was then about 10 years old. Thomas Lincoln was good-natured and honest, but he always seemed to be retreating before the approach of the comforts and advantages of a developing community. About 1800 he settled in Elizabethtown and during the next few years was a hard-working and industrious member of the community.

On June 12, 1806, he married Nancy Hanks. The couple made their home in Elizabethtown, where their first child, Sarah, was born in 1807. On December 12, 1808, Thomas Lincoln bought for $200 in cash and other obligations the 300-acre Sinking Spring farm, a few miles south. February 12, 1809 Abraham Lincoln was born in a one-room cabin near the large limestone spring of cool water for which the place was named. The humble beginning of life for the beloved 16th President of the United States is now a National Historic Site, maintained by the Department of the Interior. Today the spring is still there, gurgling plenty of water as it did in 1808 and the huge white oak tree called the Boundary Oak is some 160 years older than it was when the Lincoln family enjoyed its majestic shade. The Lincolns lived about 2 1/2 years at the Sinking Spring farm, which eventually was lost to them because of a defective land title. Before midsummer 1811 they moved to a farm on Knob Creek, about 10 miles to the northeast.

The traditional birthplace cabin was reerected within the memorial building in 1911.

Over 100,000 people contributed to the fund which built the Lincoln National Birthplace Memorial.

Until its death in 1976, the Boundary Oak was a surveyor's landmark from the days of Lincoln's birth.

Sinking Spring from which the farm was named.

Knob Creek, Kentucky

THE Knob Creek Farm was a good farm and the Lincoln family lived there from midsummer in 1811 until 1816. Abraham Lincoln's first recollections of his boyhood were from the Knob Creek Farm. Years later when he was President he was reminiscing to a visitor at the White House about how the rains in the spring would wash down the hillside and one time washed away the corn seed they had hand-planted. Abraham's only brother, Thomas, Jr., was born here, died and is buried in the Redman Family Cemetery. Young Abe and his sister, Sarah, attended their first two terms of school two miles from the Knob Creek cabin. Lincoln wrote: "The place on Knob Creek....I remember it well. My earliest recollection is of the Knob Creek place."

Autumn 1816 the Lincoln family migrated to Indiana. The Lincoln Heritage Trail follows the path taken by Thomas Lincoln and his family. It is believed the Lincoln family crossed the Ohio River slightly north of Hawesville at a point to connect with Anderson Creek Landing.

Lincoln cabin on Knob Creek.

Thomas Lincoln's growing family occupied the Knob Creek Farm for five years, 1811−1816. Abe and his sister Sarah attended their first two terms of school two miles from the Knob Creek cabin. When Thomas Lincoln had trouble over the ownership of his farm, he decided to make a new start in the state of Indiana.

Lincoln City, Indiana

IN the autumn of 1816, Thomas Lincoln and his family left Kentucky and crossed the Ohio River into Indiana. The land he picked for their new home lay south of Little Pigeon Creek in an area of wooded hills. Although he was still a young boy, Abe "was large for his age, and had an axe put in his hands at once." Soon the cabin was raised and furnished, land cleared and crops planted.

Here Abraham grew from 7 years to 21. The life was hard and after two years of struggle Nancy Lincoln died in the autumn of 1818 of the "milk sickness" on October 5. "Brilliant, intellectual, strong-minded, gentle, kind, and tender" were the words her neighbours used to describe her. These qualities she passed on to her son. The loneliness was lessened by his father's marriage to Sally Bush Johnston, a widow with children of her own. His stepmother encouraged him to study and learn while she nurtured his potential greatness. In 1830 the Lincolns sold their farm and moved to Illinois.

The Lincolns farmed the land in the painstaking manner of the day.

The Lincolns built a pioneer cabin south of Little Pigeon Creek in an area of wooded hills.

They made most of their tools and furniture.

*The Lincolns cared
for their animals
and gave them
shelter.*

*On October 5, 1818,
Nancy Lincoln died
of "milk sickness."*

The pioneer wife had to be skilled in many ways. She did her own spinning and made the clothes for her family; cooked over an open fire, washed by hand, preserved fruits by drying, worked in the garden and still found time to tend flowers and help her neighbours.

Vincennes, Indiana

THE Lincoln Memorial Bridge crosses the Wabash River at the place where the Lincoln family crossed from Indiana to Illinois in 1830. Vincennes is rich in Lincoln associations beginning with the arrival of the family in Lincoln City in 1816. Thomas Lincoln, his father, rode from Lincoln City to Vincennes and entered his farm at the United States Land Office in 1817. In 1827 he returned and surrendered half his claim and received a patent for eighty acres signed by President John Quincy Adams. No doubt Lincoln heard much about Vincennes from William Jones the proprietor of a general store near the Lincoln home. As a youth Abe clerked there.

At the time the Lincoln family migrated to Illinois they passed through Vincennes in March, 1830. Abe saw his first printing press here. Tradition says they remained there three days in order to have their wagon-ties set by a blacksmith. The migrating party included the Thomas Lincoln family, Abraham, then 21 was in this group.

The George Rogers Clark National Memorial

Lincoln Memorial Bridge spanning the Wabash River where the Lincoln family crossed over from Indiana to Illinois in 1830.

The memorial plaque is called the Lincoln Trail Monument

New Salem, Illinois

NEW SALEM is representative of hundreds of similar settlements which lived briefly as the frontier moved westward. Two years after a mill was built on the Sangamon River and the town was founded on the bluff above the Mill, Abe Lincoln, then only 22, arrived in New Salem. In the six interim years, Abe tried his hand at a variety of jobs—store clerk, mill hand, post master, storekeeper, surveyor, and soldier in the Black Hawk War. Lincoln later described himself as "like a piece of floating driftwood."

While in New Salem Abe studied endlessly, especially the law, doing his work in various of the town's log buildings including the Rutledge Tavern where he boarded and slept in the loft with the Rutledge boys. Abe was liked and respected by his neighbours who twice sent him to the State Legislature. In 1837, Lincoln borrowed a horse, threw his meager belongings into two saddle bags, and set out to practice law in Springfield. New Salem Village is now an Illinois State Memorial.

Bronze Statue by Avard Fairbanks ▶

WITH MALICE TOWARD NONE   ITH CHARITY FOR ALL

Rutledge Tavern, built by one of the founders of New Salem

New Salem welcomed the Joshua Miller blacksmith shop.

Carding Mill and Wool House, built by Samuel Hill in 1835.

Springfield, Illinois

IN April, 1837, Lincoln came to Springfield to live and to practice law. He first became the law partner of John T. Stuart, whom he had met in the Black Hawk War. In 1844, Lincoln asked William H. Herndon to join in partnership with him. He met Mary Todd in December 1839, at a ball and after a temptuous courtship, they married on November 4, 1842. Mary, a well-educated Kentuckian, was then 23 years old, and Abe Lincoln was 33.

Abraham Lincoln's Home on the corner of 8th & Jackson Streets, in Springfield is the only one he ever owned. In 1847 Lincoln was elected to Congress and served one term as a Whig Representative. When he returned to Springfield he continued his law practice and "Rode the Circuit." On May 16, 1860, in Chicago, Lincoln was nominated as the Republican candidate for the presidency. Lincoln left Springfield in February of 1861. Standing on the platform of his train, Lincoln said, "I now leave, not knowing when, or whether ever, I may return."

Abraham Lincoln's home at Eight and Jackson Streets.

The Lincoln-Herndon Law Office

Lincoln, 16th President of the United States, learned, lived and died for Law, Justice and Love of Fellowman. In 1844, Lincoln asked William H. Herndon to join in partnership with him.

The first State House in Springfield

Front Parlor of Abraham Lincoln's Home

The Lincoln tomb in Oak Ridge Cementery.

Washington, D.C.

It is hard to believe that Lincoln came to Washington as an undistinguished member of the House of Representatives. Later; out of public office, he gained stature arguing against slavery. He returned to Washington as President of a hopelessly divided country. Suffering through the war years he sometimes attended performances at Ford's Theatre. On April 9, 1865. The Confederate Army surrendered—Mrs. Lincoln made plans to attend the theatre on the evening of April 14.

''Our American Cousin'' was playing to a full house and the Lincolns were seated in the upper right hand box. The stage setting is for the third act, the point the play had reached when the President was shot. Doctors scrambled quickly into the President's box, examined his wound, pronounced it mortal, and helped to carry the unconscious leader across the street to the home of William Petersen. There, at 7:22 the following morning, Abraham Lincoln died. On February 13, 1868, Ford's Theatre was reopened to the public.

The Lincoln Memorial is located at the West End of the Mall, on the banks of the Potomac River

Daniel Chester French statue of Abraham Lincoln ▶

Ford's Theatre was opened to the public on the night of August 27, 1863. It was Washington's most successful theatre.

Colorful interior of the Ford Theatre

*John Wilkes Booth
had his last
drink here*

The house in which Lincoln died, now 516 10th Street NW., was built by William Petersen in 1849. Because the house had more rooms than they needed, the family kept roomers. William T. Clark, employed by the Quartermaster General's Office, occupied the room to which Lincoln was taken.